Grandad's Tales

Tall & True

Doug McPhillips

Also, by Doug McPhillips:

NOVELS. AND ALBUMS

From Darkness to Light
Awake to My Gutted Dreams
The Sword of Discernment
Santiago Traveller
I Prophet: towards 2030
Master's at my table
The Guru of Jerusalem
We Is Me Upside Down (Auto-biography)
The Wicklow Way
The Adventures of Ace McDice,
Stretch Deed & Moonshine Melody
Instant Karma & Grace
The Credo
Reflections of an Old Man
A Writer on the Rocks
Reincarnation of the Assassin
Master of the Arts
The Songs, not the Singer
To Whom It May Concern
New Sprouts from Old Branches
Masters of Introspection
 The Rise and Rise of a 4th Reich
  Journey to a Hermit's Haven
  A Camino Guide Book

  Country Camino (Album)
  Santiago Traveller (Album)
  Soul Fact. (Album)

Doug McPhillips March 2025

ISBN.978-1-763698376

This book is copyrighted. Except for fair dealings for private study, research, criticism, or review, as permitted under the Copyright Act, no part may be reproduced by any process without the editor's written permission.

This book is a work of fact and fiction. All characters in this novel are reprinted herein, and names of people living at the time may be fictitious. Any resemblance to actual events, locales, or persons living or dead is entirely coincidental but, where applicable, is real. Where poetic license turns fact into fiction, names have changed to protect the innocent.

For my grandchildren
and
For all children who enjoy stories.

Introduction.

I recall many images of "Pop," my grandad, from the pictures in my memory bank. The gaunt prospector, face and body drew in over the last grain of food eaten, the last drop of water drunk, and the sweat dripping from his weathered brown, digging deep into the drought-hardened earth of the desert country, still with a will to work, following a gold seam in the hope of the mother lode. Then, turning to another image, I consider the same man sitting short, squat and strong in the saddle, driving cattle across the Liverpool plains to a loading dock in far-off Western Australia, collecting his well-earned cheque for his trouble. If you can picture these images, then you have my Grandad.

There is more to his story, though, as he was the same man riding high in the saddle, cracking his stock whip as he rounded up ranging cattle in the New England Ranges for the next muster cattle drive to market. He was the same man who travelled to sheds as a sundowner, shearing sheep for a quid and showcasing his skills at a local agricultural show. At the same time, his long-standing friend Jimmy Sharman, the boxing promoter, stood outside his tent nearby, beating his drum and chanting: "Who'll pick up a glove?" Jimmy, who travelled from show to show with his Aboriginal boxing troupe, challenged the locals to fight his boxers, hoping to raise a quid or two for his efforts.

My grandad had a lifetime of stories to share about his travels; some were difficult, but more often than not, he danced and sang the night away to the distant sounds of his Irish forebears, usually tap dancing and doing an Irish Jig!

Yes, that older man was my grandad, lovingly called "Pop" by his grandchildren. He told us stories of years gone by, neatly woven from his own lifetime experiences, as he sat on his verandah in his later years, smoking the last of his "Roll me ones" and sharing tall and true tales. The years have flown by, and like my long-deceased grandad, I now sit as he once did, recounting stories of my wild and woolly youth, life experiences filled with a blend of tall tales and truth.

As I think of those days of old, many characters will come to mind, and they will appear as if by magic on the following pages. So it is for you children to glean from your imagination what you discern is real and what is just the make-believe of this older man, your grandad. For it is told here for your benefit that it may be passed on before I return to the dust from whence I came to be.

Happy memories from what I tell here for your enjoyment, good fortune, lessons learned and happy trails for you to remember for the future. Now read on…

CHAPTER 1.

GRANDAD'S YARNS

The oldest of cocks crowed at dawn as it had always done, and Grandad was up and dressed before the encore of the brood of male chooks followed the call of the leader. Pop had a quick splash of water on his face to clear the sleep from his eyes and a toilet stop outback before heading to the storage shed for some bee pollen mix of the nectar to feed his chickens for good health. Later in the day, he would feed them again with leftover vegetable scraps from the kitchen waste to give them what he considered a balanced diet.

My old 'Pop' still maintained a spritely step in his dotage, hardened by hard work in his younger days. More to that shortly, but back to his morning ritual. After feeding the chooks, Grandad headed to the lemon trees to pick the best fruit of the bitter lemon for his health. He always maintained that the nectar of lemon juice was a cure-all remedy for most ills. First, he felt for the ripest of lemons and picked two from the best trees in the grove. Going inside, Pop would make himself a hot lemon drink before breakfast. If he felt poorly, he would boil a handful of lemons, drink the juice, and eat the stewed-up reminder for good measure. On other occasions, he was known to squeeze raw lemon juice on an open wound to kill bacteria. Grandad was never known to use any other medicine for illness, except when he needed to top off his night with a good stiff brandy before retiring.

Interestingly, Grandad believed what he fed the chickens was good enough for him to eat for breakfast. So, he would mix the pollen with a cup of boiled milk and eat it. He then drank tea from a kettle of boiling water heated over an old fuel stove. While drinking his tea, he would toast a slice of bread with a long fork on the open fireplace and eat it topped with honey from his bee hives.

The kitchen stove generated a lot of heat in that tiny kitchen as the family gathered and huddled together to eat breakfast in winter. The heat was stifling in summer, so my grandmother prepared breakfast for the family, who adjourned to the dining table, awaiting a feast of bacon and eggs, tea, and toast with butter and jam or honey.

The early morning ritual included listening to the ABC news on the radio and the forever episodes of "Blue Hills" by Gwen Meredith. The series was a daily 15-minute episode of a story that revolved around 'The Lawsons' farming family and lasted from 1949 to 1976 with a total of 5,795 episodes; it was the longest-running radio series ever. It was for my grandmother Nana's distraction while scrubbing the kitchen bench and dining room table after hand-washing all the dishes. She followed this by storing the weekly meat quota in a tiny gauze wire box safe from flies as it hung in a breezeway near the back door. There was also an ice chest for food cooling, with a large block of ice delivered once a week by a vendor. It was many years before modern-day refrigeration came into being. Nana always kept the ice chest topped up with vegetables from the garden when not preserving fruit in jars or making jams. Grandad's primary duty apart from the chooks was to tend to his fruit trees, which mainly composed his precious lemons; Grandad had no other animals to care for once he retired, save for the chooks. I reckon he had enough sheep, dogs, horses and cattle in his farming and droving days to last him a lifetime.

Once breakfast was over, Granddad made his way to the front verandah, where he took pride of place, seated on a well-worn wooden stool. There, he lit a 'roll me own' cigarette after stuffing one end into his homemade holder, puffing away to his heart's content. Grandad needed this initial time to reflect on his former life. He waited for his grandchildren to sit by his feet, and once settled, he began to tell a story or two. My Grandad Barney was always 'Pop' to us children. He was the most excellent raconteur and had stories gleaned from a colourful lifetime as a drover, mailman, gold prospector, sheepherder, shearer, timber cutter, and farmer.

Pop's eight grandchildren, including me, re-acquainted once a year at Christmas as we gathered to hear another story. In our eyes, he was like the Pied Piper of Hamilton, and his cheerful nature and quick mind mesmerised us from the moment he began to tell a tale. I remember a particular morning when all my cousins had left. I was the only one seated on the verandah, anxiously eager to hear another story from Grandad's memory bank. A couple of local ring-ins appeared at the end of the verandah, wanting to join in. Grandad looked at them sternly, took out his pocket knife, opened the blade, and pointed it at them: " I saw you both taking fruit from my lemon trees without asking my permission. Is that right?" The two boys, no more than six years of age or so, stood with heads lowered and nodded in unison. Once Grandad had their undivided attention and mine, he announced: "If I ever catch you doing that again, I will cut you up into tiny pieces, put you in a sack, tie the top in a knot with string and take you down to the river and drown you." He pauses as he points to the open blade and says: "Is that understood?" Like those little boys, we never questioned Pop's logic regarding such weighty matters as his precious lemon trees and his fondness for the bitter fruit. That juice was the miracle liquid to cure all, besides a brandy or two to help him sleep at night. By some miracle, the medical marvel with lemons had always worked for my Grandad. He closed the pocket knife's blade, put it in his pocket, and returned to tell a tale to those repentant, former lemon tree thieves and me.

My favourite yarn of Pop's tales was the one he told of his days looking for water during a drought using a water divider. It was a method called drowsing, using two twigs, one in each hand, that pulled down hard towards the ground where some treasure would be uncovered. It was historically a sacred way for underground water to be found. Drowsing, as it is known, is employed even today by those who have ' the gift' to locate underground water, buried metal or ores, gemstones, oil, gravesites, and even rivers of gold without using scientific apparatus.

Before Pop mastered the art of a water divider, Y-shaped twigs were employed. It was enormously popular in Germany in the 16th century for profound mining practitioners who had 'the gift' became in high demand throughout Europe and Elizabethan England. It was used effectively in Elizabeth's royal mines from calamine then and in silver mines in Wales. It was in the admirable life of St.Teresa of Spain that in 1568, she was offered a site for a convent, but there was no water supply there. Happily, Friar Antonio came with a twig in hand, stopped at a particular spot, appeared to be making a sign of the cross with the twig and, in her own words, "Really, I can't be sure if it were the sign of the cross he made with that twig. At any rate, he moved with the twig and said, ' Dig here. ' So they dug, and a plentiful water supply gushed forth, excellent for drinking, copious for washing and never ran dry.' Teresa, not having ever heard of dowsing, considered it a miracle.

At any rate, Pop considered he had 'the gift' of finding water. The land was desperate and in drought back then, as it often is today. So, I guess he used two twigs to search for water on his land.

Well, as with all of Pop's recounting of his experiences, he coloured it with style and Irish baloney to keep his little ones at his feet all ears, as he told of using two twig rods all day and into the darkness of night in a desperate bid to find water. Pop said to us that he had all but given up hope, and as it was far too late to return to the homestead, he decided to make camp for the night. So he tied his horse to a nearby tree, rolled out his swag and blanket for a bed, and lit a fire to cook some tucker he carried in his knapsack.

To bring realism into his reliving the story, Grandad picked up two twigs in the garden and demonstrated how he had both twigs in hand the night he camped, when suddenly the twigs turned downwards toward the fire. The use of Twigs was always a telltale sign of something lying beneath the surface, and it is how a good dowser could feel the pull on the twigs that set alarm bells going in his head. Grandad said: " I decided then and there to put out the fire and dig to see what lay below."

Grandad had a pregnant pause for a moment, as good raconteurs often do in telling tales, then he continued: " To my surprise, appeared a large boulder of pure gold ore." Then Grandad Pop's baloney of a story reached a new dimension. After a couple of puffs of his smoke, he continued: " I dug and dug and could not reach the bottom of the mountain of gold, so I just cut off a piece as a sample to take to a buyer in the morning to determine the purity of my find." By this time, our overactive minds were in awe of Pop's fine, but somehow, I suspected he was making it all up. "How did you know it was gold, Pop; it was dark, wasn't it, when you found it once the fire was out?' I reasoned. I could see the glint in his eye as he rolled another 'roll em own,' cleaned out his cigarette holder with the small blade knife he had threatened to cut up the lemon thieves, placed the neatly rolled cigarette in the holder, lit the end with a match stick and began to smoke. In a slow but contemplative mood, he replied,
" You doubt your old Pop's words, boy?' Before I had time to feel ashamed for questioning the truth of his story, Grandad reached deep into his trouser pocket, pulled out

an old rag of a handkerchief, unfolded it, and behold, was a solid piece of gold right there. "This is the piece I just told you about that I had analysed. It is pure 22-carat and worth a fortune, and I own a mountain of the stuff." Of course, his story was not true, but he always had the ammunition to verify it, and I always believed him.

I remember one Christmas Eve when I was about five or six. Grandad woke me after midnight that Christmas to follow Santa Claus. We crept around the house in the dark with a torchlight, looking for clues about where Santa was putting out the Christmas gifts. Pop led me into the lounge, whispered that he could see Santa near the fireplace, and convinced me in the dim light of his torch that I could see him if I looked hard enough. " Look, there he goes." He said, "See, he has just put the presents in front of the fireplace." And sure enough, the family's gifts were by the fireplace and at the foot of my parents' bed.

"Quick, Dougie", Pop called when he distracted me for a moment: "Look." he whispered: "Look, Santa's heading up the chimney." Pop moved stealthily to the fireplace with me close in pursuit and quickly stuck his hand up the chimney and exclaimed: " I've got him by his beard." I was excited, but joy turned to disappointment when Pop said: " Dash, he got away." He pulled out his hand and showed me that he had pulled out some of Santa's beard. It was cotton wool, but in the dim light of that lounge room, it looked like the real thing. I wanted to pocket it, but Pop said it was a treasure and had to be kept in safe keeping with the piece of gold for future reference. It was not until Pop had long passed to the other side that reason took precedence over the imagination. When cleaning out his bedside drawers, the gold piece and Santa's cotton wool beard were again discovered.

There were many stories by my Grandad of his droving days, horseback pony express rides delivering mail, rounding up sheep shearing and time with fellow drovers and long trail rides. I could relate to many of his exploits here, but I prefer to revert to poems I've written that tell of Grandad's exploits better than I tell lengthy stories. I want to repeat some of my grandpa's lifestyles in poetic utterances.

Well, I've been a boundary rider,
on the wild New England range,
rounded up range cattle,
driven more across the plains.

Oh! I learned to live in the bush when I was just a kid,
camping out with my granddad,
cutting the timbers, what he did.

I've had my share of hard times,
I've had my fill of pain, If I had my time back over,
I'd do it all again.

Killing dingoes when in danger,
cooking rabbit to survive,
staying warm at night log fire,
sleeping out when I was five.

Well, I crossed the barren desert,
and I tramped the hills alone,
made it through some swollen rivers,
wild dust storms and chilly snows.

Cause I've been an overlander,
it was the life I'd lived,
If I had my time back over,
I'd do it all again.

Well, my Granddad was a drover,
cross the country he did roam,
seeking out his heart's companion,
where he found his heart and home.

Boxed in tents for Jimmy Sharman,
tried to earn a decent quid,
carried swag across the Darling,
seeking work, that's what he did.

He cut timber on the north coast,
drove cattle on the plain,
shore sheep west of Tamworth,
In those good old country days.

Panned for gold in old Kalgoorlie,
strut the boards and sang on stage,
did his share of hard-core drinking,
In the good old country ways.

Once he sat on his verandah,
telling stories to grandkids,
of the life he'd left behind him,
and the things that he once did.

So I sing this song for Grandad,
in my heart, he will remain,
cause he was a boundary rider,
on the wild New England range.

"Hear the thunder on the mountain,
It's the brumbies on the run,
see the murder of the black crow,
as they greet the morning sun."

"Feel the gentle chill of first light,
tea and damper are almost done,
breaking camp, we long to start out,
saddle up for boundary run".

There's a child who sat beside him,
On the day that he had died,
He came back for a moment,
then he rode off with a smile,

Chasing moonbeams in the starlight,
somewhere in the sky above,
looking down on boundary riders,
With a heart stocked full of love.

Well, he'd been a boundary rider,
on the wild New England range,
rounded up range cattle,
driven more across the plains.

He had his share of hard times,
had his fill of pain,
If he had his time back over,
He'd probably do it all again.

"Hear the thunder on the mountain,
it's the brumbies on the run,
see the murder of the black crow,
as they greet the morning sun.

Feel the gentle chill of the first light
tea and damper almost done,
breaking camp, we long to start,
Saddle up for boundary run."

Oh! He had his share of heartache,
had his fill of pain,
If he had his time back over,
He'd probably do it all again.

Here, you can draw something related to the characters in the stories. Use a grey pencil or coloured crayon to add to this story.

CHAPTER 2

TALES FROM YOUR GRANDAD

Your grandad wrote many poetic tales about his grandad, Barney. However, as I mentioned, he was best known as "Pop" to us children. Here are some stories in poetry format for your reading pleasure. I hope you like them.

The Last Stockman.

Old Barney was my grandad,
He had many a tale to tell,
some were happy and sad,
Others were just fables!

He told of a sad, sad story
of an old stockman named Ned,
it was in the wild Mallee country,
about the day the stockman died.

Well, the sun dawned slowly,
on that misty dust dull dawn,
spreading eastern rays
across the sluggish land.

It was Ned's last dreaming morning,
on his precious cattle trail,
were the sun shot a flaming pathway,
to view the sand peaks blazed.

The bleary-eyed stockman
were saddling up to break camp,
they were holding onto their horses
to bridle up and saddle.

They were starting the muster,
to drive the cattle across the land,
finished their last tea and damper,
To let out across the plain.

Old Ned stepped from the saddle,
and he went when nature called,
Squat down by a Mallee scrub,
It was the only tree about.

Old Ned yelled out a holler,
" The bastards bit my ass,"
As the cunning brown snake hid
beneath the tree, that evil asp!

Well, Ned, he cursed and grumbled,
 as he got up on his horse,
he had treated the wound as best he could,
for who could bandage a bitten ass?

Oh! They drove the cattle all that day,
Til Ned called out to Barney,
" See that old tree up ahead,
I'd like to cut a branch off,
make a hook and sink the sun."

Barney, my old grandad, in a joke,
Said matter-of-factly:
"I'd rather cut a 'Y' fork
Prop up the sun for longer,
Finish the cattle drive and collect my pay."

To the South, the sand hills blazing,
to the West a bridle path,
that led to a bluff,
at the side of the first hill,
a place to camp at last!

It was a perfect campsite,
not far from the driving stop,
near tea trees on a pathway,
where eucalyptus grow a lot.

"Well, lift me from the saddle", cried Ned,
Old friend, I am on my last,
You did well to guide my horse,
now the asp's poison has taken its grasp."

He smiled as he lay there dying,
remembering times that last,
dreaming of years in the saddle,
Telling an old tale of the past.

"Oh! I remember a glowing morning,
Out on the gleaming grass,
we watched our cool tobacco clouds,
watched the white wreaths pass."

"We sat loosely in the saddle,
As we herded the cattle in yards,
Rang the fire of our stock whips raging,
In the fiery run of hooves."

"We were a glowing band of drovers,
as we rode the sun-dried land,
The flint stone echoed the ranges,
were the cattle stampede rang,

Close behind them, through ten tea trees,
through the golden timbered fern,
Beneath the weeping willows,
We trapped them in a gorge."

"Yeah, we were the best of men." cried Ned,
In his dying breath,
You were riding the chestnut Barney,
And me, the old grey horse."

"We emptied flaming six-shooters,
Rode the chestnut and the grey,
And we cracked our whips,
till the steers were done,
man to man, we won the day."

Now, old Ned began to pray,
as they watched him slip away,
so they buried him by an old gum tree,
under rocks to keep dingoes at bay.

Barney returned to the place where the asp bit Ned,
He turned over every rock and stick,
till he found that snake at last.

So he loaded up his shotgun,
and he blew the snake away,
Grandad always wore snake-skin boots,
from that very day.

Now the wheat grows where once was cattle,
no more cattle on the plain,
Long haul trucks carry them to market,
And dams where once there was rain.

There bloom tea trees and the wattle,
they were once they could not grow
There are trains now full of iron ore,
They were the cattlemen who once rode the plain.

Oh! The deep blue skies wax dusty,
tall grass grows on the plain,
were the smoky sinking shadows
hide the sleeping sunlight rays.

Let me slumber in the hollow,
were the white blossoms waving,
with never a stone nor rail to fence me in,
put bush flowers upon my grave.

Just for now, let me live in the sunshine,
walk in the wind and rain,
carry my knapsack and tucker bag,
to see where the last stockman was laid.

Cause I guess when the final time will come,
like it does to every man,
I will end up with Barney, my grandad,
And I will go where most men go.

Grandad has had many adventures with old friend Larry, the animal veterinarian, and another named "Barefoot Bob" because he never wore boots or sneakers. The story is more about another Bob, Bobbie Beer, Mountaineer, another friend of mine.

Here is a story of a wild mountaineer,
goes by the name of Bobby Beer,
He never walked a mountain track,
Nor did he tramp a valley floor,
He'd just run up and down them.

(And he ran like Clancy rode them.)

Oh! I've walked with Larry the Vet,
On many a mountain climb,
Strode out with barefoot Bob,
He died… He was a friend of mine.

We often traversed difficult paths,
some were steep and rugged to climb,
but we never had the strength,
stamina or prowess, the way Bobby Beer did when he ran.

It was in the spring of eighty,
It was when I first met Bob,
He was working on a contract
for some government survey mob.

They were working in the Apsley Gorge
planning to build a dam,
giving a boost to our electricity needs,
but the country went into recession,
Premier Wran abandoned the plan.

The gorge is at the mouth of the Apsley,
with a thousand-metre drop,
The workers had built a track down,
To drive four-wheelers down to the job.

Bobby Beer never rode, always ran it,
Starting at the very top,
He would run right down to the valley bottom,
and then run right back up to the top.

Now I know that a thousand meters drop,
a sad and lonely spot,
a friend and I moved a boulder from there,
and we pushed it over the top.

It was at that point our white ancestors
rounded up three hundred men,
full-blooded Aboriginals,
forced them to jump the gorge.

Now, that's a sad, sad story.
the history books don't tell,
I have a copy of the testament,
of three hundred Aboriginal murders,
where our rock boulder silently fell.

For that's another story.,
one not taught in school,
of the death of many black brothers,
when they taught us mushroom rules.

Now, I am getting away from Bobby's story,
for the other can wait another day;
this one is about the wild mountain man,
how he crossed the Simpson Desert
 a decade or two yesterday.

Let's take a break and have a beer. Before I tell you more of a story:

" So, raise your glasses
 and be of good cheer,
and drink a drink,
to Bobby Beer!"

When Bobby had been running,
He disappeared for a week,
in those wild New England Ranges
living on berries and water from a creek.

Bobby turned up at the end of June,
on a bitterly cold winter's day,
He was wearing untied laced work boots,
football shorts and a torn old shirt.

He came to borrow my paper,
said he was catching a train west,
 but I never knew until later
It was the Simpson desert quest.

It was Friday 29th July, 1980,
Bobby Beer crossed our barren land,
In six days, six hours and thirty,
He set a record back then.

Now, the township of Birdsville,
quite near the Birdsville track,
had a day of celebration
The day Bobby Beer got back.

"So, raise your glasses,
Be of good cheer,
and drink a drink,
To Bobby Beer."

He told the newspapers
of the sand hills, three storeys high,
how he fell,
He sprained his ankle and tore his thigh!

Now, other men had tried the feat
that Bobby lived to tell,
Like Warren Boughton, a scientist,
Who knew the desert well.

Broughton crossed the desert.
In twenty-eight days,
with an entire backup crew,
For they had plenty of water
dropped in from an aeroplane.

So many have tried the desert walk,
many have died as well,
like the Frenchman Fatin in seventy-six,
He was never seen again.

Bobby crossed the desert in record time,
living on water, milk and juice,
He had little backup for his feat,
cause he lost his backup crew.

Dick Smith of electronics fame,
He flew his helicopter in,
When he heard of Bobby's feat,
He was keen to interview him.

Bobby didn't want the fame;
He hid behind the Apsley hotel,
stayed in the dark, drinking champagne,
He just wanted to be left alone.

Now, many others have tried the feat,
to beat old Bobby's time,
But I think Pat Farmer did it
in some new record time.

Oh! The last time I saw Bobby Beer,
he looked a little worse for wear,
It was at the Country Music Fair,
arm in arm with dark Susie Green.

Well, it's been over three decades,
Since Bobby became a folk hero,
I just lost track of him,
on some mountain track, I tramped.

Thinking back on those days gone by,
as I tramp along,
and whilst I've given up drinking days,
I say to those who do:

"Raise your glasses,
Be of good cheer,
and drink a drink,
to Bobby Beer."

You can create one or two more drawings on this page and the next.

CHAPTER 3.

GREAT GRANDAD

Now we've travelled through some of the stories of my grandad, 'Pop.' He was your great-great-grandfather, and my dad, Eric, was your great-grandfather. So I can't leave him out of the story, for if you don't know about his life and times, then the gift of his life will be forgotten for good. By the way, Eric means 'Prince,' which he was to me.

Old Barney, my "Pop," whilst spending the better part of his life as a single man on horseback driving cattle, and when the jobs dried up, he went prospecting for gold. The horseback mail delivery job from Tablelands to Grafton on the North Coast was his last time in the saddle as a single man. Pop ultimately settled into the life of a sheep farmer on a small holding in what was known as the 'eighteen-mile' from Grafton. He had married my grandmother Isabella and thought it best to have a more stable life and bring up his brood of seven children, six boys and a girl. Dad was the youngest of twins, and whilst the other boys relished living on a sheep farm, your great-grandfather did not like it. Interestingly, none of Dad's brothers stayed on the land, preferring occupations like timber getters, fishermen, and publicans. My aunty married a racehorse breeder, so neither she nor my uncle was interested in the property. When "Pop" died and the property was sold, Dad declined to take any of the money from the sale. He told his brothers and sister to keep his share, as he was never interested in being a sheep station owner and reasoned that he wasn't entitled to benefit from the sale.

The only reminder of the property's existence is the bridge near the old Pacific Highway, which still bears the sign.
" McPhillips' Bridge." Nearby, at the northern entrance to the timber forest, the signpost says "McPhillips track," which tells little about the life and times of my family's bloodline.

Eric, my Dad and your great-grandfather have always had a keen interest in music. He learnt the piano as a boy, walked the lone distance from the sheep station five miles to the township of Grafton and back to get piano lessons, and did odd jobs to eventually purchase his piano, which held pride of place in our lounge room when I was a child. I, too, learnt to play the piano as a child, but I didn't like the practice, preferring to be running around the bush or playing games with my mates. So, I gave it up in high school and have regretted it ever since. It would have made my songwriting easier because your old granddad often writes songs now in his dotage.

Dad initially considered being a butcher in his youth, as he saw the meat-eating public forever at the butcher shop getting their cut of beef or lamb. In my Grandad 'Pops' working life, most jobs entailed working on horseback. Still, with the increase after WW11 in the public's desire to own a motor car, and as trucks began to replace horse-drawn vehicles, Dad soon reasoned that motor mechanics was the new career for his future. He turned his mind to study, becoming Dux, the top pupil in his school, and ultimately studied mechanical engineering, working initially in Grafton and later working his way up to head engineer for a business on the North Coast, which he ultimately purchased and developed into the most prominent truck servicing business from Newcastle to the Queensland border. Mum was the dutiful wife who gave up her working life early. They were both twenty-one when they married, and I came along a year later.

His story could take a typical journey of a self-made man's journey in building his empire, only to see it all crumble to dust. I think his exploits outside of working hours are more humorous and serve to tell his devil-may-care attitude of being more of interest and abilities beyond the everyday run-of-the-mill hard-working man. Dad often talked of some of his early exploits as a junior mechanic. A couple of those incidents come to mind when I recall his storytelling.

One New Year's night, when Dad was having a few drinks with a neighbour, one thing that came to mind as the most interesting was when all the staff, except the junior mechanics, were invited to a local business Christmas party. Dad was peeved about it as he was not invited and decided with one of his mechanic mates to make the party attendees pay for their indiscretion. He took another mate, Mick Denham, as 'cockatoo,' a lookout for his pending prank. All three had made their way to the businessman's home, where the party was progressing. It was agreed that Mick would jump the back fence and check that no one could identify the two young mechanics when they went into prank mode. As fate would have it, when Mick jumped the wall, who should be on the other side but a vicious German shepherd guard dog? Mick had primed himself with enough alcohol before this endeavour to have no fear of the consequences and immediately dropped to the ground and, on all fours, advanced towards the approaching growling dog. The two met face to face in a split second, and Mick out-growled the savage beast. The dog backed off, and Mick kept advancing towards the animal, still on all fours and barking wildly. Eventually, the dog headed for its kennel, and Mick checked the back and front of the house before returning to the pranksters, ready to give the all-clear. The cars of the mid-1940s were open with wind-up windows or canvas see-through side windscreens, so it was not an issue for the two young mechanics to set each car up for the prank.

Back then, cars had manual gear sticks, and the hand brake was the only other safety feature that required metal squeezing a trigger-like handle to put in drive mode. The two pranksters wired the metal hand to the battery so the driver would get an electric shock when the car started.
After setting each car belonging to the partygoers in this fashion, they returned to the next task. They took the jacks from each car and put the jack under the axle so that the back wheels were slightly off the ground but undetectable to the naked eye. They had only just completed their endeavour when the first car owner returned to his car. He started his motor and attempted to release the hand brake while letting out an almighty scream. He swore and tried to reverse the car, but the wheels spun, and he was stuck. He returned inside to tell his fellow partygoers what had happened. In a matter of minutes, all the drivers were

trying to figure out how to get the car moving, and many in their cars fell into the trap of attempting to let the handbrake off after starting the motor. Vehicle wheels were left spinning, but the cars remained stationary, and drivers were perplexed and scratching their heads. It was a cloudy night with the party revelers primed with alcoholic beverages; they had no choice but to return to retrieve their cars in the morning. Dad and his two companions sat behind a fence across the road and had trouble containing laughter. Clive Sayer related the story about his car the next day to all and sundry, but he was none the wiser, as it was Dad and his fellow employee who had done the ghastly deeds.

One Christmas holiday period, Dad and our next-door neighbour, Ron, hatched a plan to throw a New Year's party. So Ron and Dad headed off to get a few mates and businesspeople to attend. It was the way they went about it that was intriguing. Firstly, Dad enlisted Trevor, a friend already in bed with his new bride, Jean. Dad used some means of convincing Trevor that it was an urgent matter, so he quickly dressed, and the threesome headed off to collect Don Aleman from his bed. Don was in his PJs and was one of Dad's employees, so he did what the boss asked. Dad told him not to worry, just come quickly as it was an important event. Mum was already busy preparing food and leftover Christmas pudding and cake for the revellers. The dye was cast, and capturing the menfolk continued until about one o'clock in the morning. It got so that they didn't bother explaining anything to the kidnap victim. They just rang the doorbell of the unsuspecting male resident and captured him returning to our home with another batch of people to eat, drink and be merry. By dawn, a large group of men dressed in evening suits, others with just the bottoms of their PJs and others dressed in shorts and T-shirts, were well in their cups and enjoying the revelry. Somehow, they all found their way home. Dad had fallen asleep, and my dutiful mother was left to clean up the mess.

As a boy, I often travelled with the Macksville Gift professional athletics committee, and my cousin Kay would accompany the men. Even as a teen, she could make men feel at ease in her company. Dad was the Secretary of the committee, and Trevor, a good friend, was the race starter who used a double-barrel sawn-off shotgun to start each race. The second barrel was fired when an athlete jumped the gun, trying to get a head start. It was a serious business as a lot of money was riding on each race, and all runners were on a handicap basis, so there was no favouritism. Professional athletics were state-wide events. They were called 'Gifts' as the prize money for the winners was a gift for those times of low wages.

The story goes that all are staying at the Gilgandra Hotel for their Athletics Gift Carnival. Meeting at breakfast, Kay asked for a glass of water and remarked to the waitress that the water tasted strange. The waitress replied that it was boring water from under the ground, and Kay quickly retorted: "Gosh, you sure don't waste much of the pig around here, do you." She was always quick, and we enjoyed our drinking together, too.

On this occasion, the members of the Macksville Gift attended the Gunnedah Gift. Trevor, the race starter, and his Dad Jim, the driver to and from events, who, like my father, was a founding member of the Gift, stayed together at a Gunnedah hotel with my cousin Kay. It was Sunday morning, and people in the street were going to church or getting the Sunday papers from the nearby news agency. The four intrepid travellers had breakfast, loaded Jim's car and were about ready to leave when Kay and Dad came up with an idea to have some fun before leaving town. What happened next was Dad pretending to act violently, which was out of character. He had physically appeared to have captured Kay and made a lot of noise in the street.

Meanwhile, Kay let out a merciless scream loud enough to wake the dead and all the patrons of the hotel, attracting considerable attention from the street. The men wore Bonny and Clyde-style suits with Panama hats tilted at the brim over their foreheads. Kay also donned a 1920s-inspired outfit, complete with a stylish hat. As the morning church crowd passed by, Dad opened the car's back door, seemingly tossing Kay onto the back seat before jumping in after her as she slammed the door, calling out to Jim, " Hit it, Leftie." Jim immediately pressed the accelerator, causing the car tyres to scream and burn rubber as they got away. Trevor pointed the shotgun skyward outside the window as the car pulled away from the curb and discharged both barrels. The noise and chaos triggered a crowd response, sending people running in all directions away from the scene. The incident made the local press, and Gunnedah has never been the same on a Sunday morning since that day. That was typical of the McPhillips clan for as long as I can remember.

Another incident I recall as a teenager on school holidays was when I managed to travel with Dad and a group of athletes to the Gift at Dorrigo. There was always a load of prize money to be won at these Gift carnivals. As I previously mentioned, they were professional events. Dad, with Trevor and his sidekick shotgun, ventured up the Waterfall Way for the events in the company of local athletes. We travelled to Dad's utility, which was usually used to carry truck parts or defunct engines to the local tip. We left home before sunrise in the back of the ute, several hopeful sprinters had trained under Paul Lawson, a skilled rugby league football player who later proved to be a grand coach of professional runners. As we crossed the low bridge below the Dorrigo mountain, Trevor, encouraged by Dad, put the shotgun out the window, pointed it skyward as he traditionally had done for starting races and let go of both barrels. The half-asleep runners in the back almost had heart attacks. Both Trevor and Dad could not stop laughing.

The Macksville Gift Professional Athletic Club was the first NSW Gift carnival to run professional foot racing for prize money. In my research for writing on the subject of the Club, I found this opening statement in the inaugural 1953 Gift programme's opening paragraph: "The year 1953…will dwell in the memories of all Australians for all time. It was the year Queen Elizabeth 11 was crowned, the year the Korean War ended and the election of war hero Dwight D. Eisenhower to the position of President of the

United States. We lost to England on the cricket field for the first time in 20 years. America entered the international Rugby league, and just as the year 1878 lives in memory as the introduction of the Stawell Gift in Victoria, 1953 will live as the year of the introduction of the Macksville Gift in New South Wales."

Then, with the success of the Macksville Gift in the ensuing six years, the following opening statement on the programme. "Perhaps of all the six years passed in the interim, this current year is quite the most momentous, for it marks a period of interchange of visits between leaders. Our Queen and Prince Philip visited Canada, and the U.S.A. British Prime Minister MacMillan has seen President Eisenhower and Soviet Prime Minister Khrushchev in their countries. Now, Prime Minister Khrushchev has visited Britain and the U.S.A. The programme continued: "The objectives of all these visitors and visits are the preservation of world peace and the end of the 'Cold War.' 1959 may go down in history as the year of the peacemakers and the world of these leaders acclaimed for all time. With the majority of people in the world, we hope fervently for these achievements, which, amongst other things, will allow us all to concentrate our minds and activities on the best things in life- including good sportsmanship- and promote the ideals which will take us Ever Onward!"

For my life, I wonder why Dad mixed memories of the Queen, Prime Minister, and Presidents, the Korean War aftermaths and the Cold War as introductory programmes for a professional athletic event, but he did. His duties as a young mechanic or enemy plane spotter during WW11 set him off. Or maybe it was the Korean War when he released one of his mechanics for military service, or perhaps it was the fact that he was a patriot and a real socialist at heart. His belief became even more staunch when Bob Hawke headed up the unions and Don Dunstan was elected Premier of South Australia. Despite being a relatively large employer in a small business, one would think he would have supported The Country Party or the Liberals. Still, he was 'dyed in the wool' left of the political spectrum. Dad firmly believed in unionism and was a businessman of extraordinary ability; his labour persuasion seemed out of character. Dad also put his money where his mouth was as a generous philanthropist and a man of action. At any rate, he was a grand promoter of sport and a great supporter of athletics, surf and golf clubs, being patron of all three. He attended regular monthly meetings of the local Labor Party and had me participate as the youngest member at 16 during my holiday vacation.

Eric, the Prince, a leading businessman who never stopped working, the schoolboy champion swimmer who patronised the surf club but never went to the beach. From its humble beginnings, the Golf Club patron who never played golf and the charitable donor to all the local religions who never went to Church proved himself as a successful business and first Secretary foundation member of the Macksville Gift Committee. Dad saw life as a glass half full and lived the "Ever Onward" motto of the annual athletic event daily. The Athletic Club still carries the motto, which owes as much to my father's brilliance and enthusiasm for its success as it does to its other founders. Not only does the annual event promote local charities, but it has also made the town a tourist attraction.

On the next page, draw a sketch of your great-great-grandfather or one of the other characters in this book, your old grandad.

CHAPTER 4.

PLEASANT RECALLS

My earliest memories of my father's absence from home are of frequent business trips to the Big Smoke, Sydney. He used to catch the North Coast Mail train at night, securing a first-class ticket with a sleeper—a bunk on board—to get a good night's sleep.

A "sleeper" was a compartment on the train with a fold-down bed from the wall of a private compartment, a fold-down sink that came out for fresh water, and a mirror for shaving. The bed was made up by the train guard, who happened to be a local by the name of Miley McCulluck. He was known as the " Black Mariah" because he was always dressed in black, a familiar garb for a railway employee. I guess because he was responsible for putting first-class passengers to bed and giving them a hot cup of tea before they retired, he acquired the name. It also paralleled the old horse-drawn hearses carriages for burials in the former decades; the name stuck with Miley.

My special delight in those train trips of my father, your great-grandad, was that he always returned with the latest Phantom comic book for me to read. The Phantom recounted the adventures of a crime fighter who wore a skin-tight costume and a mask that displayed white eyes who appeared in New York riding a white horse called " Hero accompanied by his faithful wolf, whom he had trained called " Devil", who was part wolf. The Phantom wore a ring that he used to knock out evil men, leaving a skull mark on the offender's cheek. In the comic strip, the

Phantom was 21st in a line of crime fighters, which began in 1536, when the father of British sailor Christopher Walker was killed during a pirate attack. Swearing an oath on the skull of his father's murderer to fight evil, Christopher began a legacy of the Phantom, which would pass from father to son. Nicknames for the Phantom include "The Ghost Who Walks", "Guardian of the Eastern Dark", and "The Man Who Cannot Die." Many other make-believe characters have existed since The Phantom, but those comic book stories inspired my imagination as a small boy.

There were occasions when Dad took me along with him on those train trips, especially when he had to collect a new imported vehicle from the Sydney docks, drive it from Sydney to his engineering workshop on the Mid-North Coast, and prepare it for the sale customers. It was no easy task, for the cars came from England by ship in the 1950s. There were no containers back then; the vehicles were tied down on the boat's deck and covered in bitumen to protect them from ocean spray. Dad would clean the front of the windscreen, back, and side mirrors and drive the vehicle on a twenty-four-hour journey north. A limited number of bridges were on the way, which meant we were carried by punt (boat) across many rivers to continue the journey. On arrival at Dad's garage, a team of workers would cut back the tar on the vehicle to the paint skin and polish it to showroom condition in readiness for the next customer. In my early childhood years, I watched as your great-grandfather imported cars, trucks, tractors and farm implements. All involved that long journey north on the old Pacific Highway. Much of the roadway was just bush track, but as time passed, the Highway improved, bridges replaced punts, and what once took a twenty-four-hour journey soon enough could be driven within eight hours.

Unlike modern-day cars that utilise a battery to power the starter motor, or hybrid engines that operate with a combination of batteries and internal combustion, the vehicles of my childhood predated computer technology and were entirely manual. They featured a straightforward four-cylinder engine connected to a drive shaft to turn the wheels, and a gear stick that needed to be shifted by the engine's revolutions. These cars required more regular maintenance, including changing the motor oil, greasing the drive fittings for each wheel, and manually replacing the brake pads. Before introducing electric starters, drivers would use a crank-shaped handle to turn over the engine. The driver was responsible for checking the brakes, the fan belt that powered the motor, and ensuring the radiator was filled with water to keep the engine cool. They also had to verify that the battery contained adequate levels of water and acid since the lead plates would eventually fail if not submerged. The final task involved ensuring the tyres were inflated to the correct pressure before setting off. Can you imagine a modern-day driver undertaking such extensive efforts for the upkeep and safety of a vehicle before heading to their destination?

I drove tractors for my dad to the market before I had a licence. When I learned to drive, it was in an old Blitz truck used by the Australian military and other Commonwealth forces during and after World War II. These trucks were also utilised in forestry, agriculture, transportation, and engineering. It was an early model of the Opel Blitz ("Lightning"), which originated in Germany and was used during WWII. Dad probably traded it in for a customer looking for a new truck; I don't recall, but it was the vehicle he taught me to drive when I obtained my licence at 16 years and 7 months.

All cars had a manual gearbox for changing gears and driving. The vehicle featured a gear stick on the floor, a clutch pedal for the left foot, and an accelerator and brake pedal for the right foot. To drive a manual car, one must press the clutch to the floor with the left foot while changing gears and accelerating with the right foot, or pressing the brake pedal to slow down or stop. This was the case for all vehicles except for the Blitz and tractors, which required a technique known as double-clutching. With this method, instead of pushing the clutch in once and directly shifting to another gear, the driver shifts the transmission into neutral before moving to the next gear, depressing and releasing the clutch with each change. I learnt to change gears using a simple heel-and-toe action, relying on the engine's sound to determine when to engage the gears. Nowadays, with automatic cars, it feels so natural as there is no need to shift gears. It is simply starting the vehicle without a gear stick, just steering and using two pedals on the floor: one to accelerate and one to help slow down or stop the car. And as for you, my grandchildren, it won't be long before we have driverless cars in the future. Change can be good, but the old days of your Granddad were fun, too.

The way to get news in the 1950s was by listening to the radio or getting yesterday's news by reading the local paper. As for the local daily gossip, there was the telephone. Owning a home phone was common for most folk. It was linked by wire cable to a local telephone exchange, and a handle on the phone could be turned to signal the telephonist at the other end who operated a switchboard. The caller would nominate two-digit numbers to the person in the district to make the call, too. The telephonist then dialled the number requested and switched the connection line between both parties. When my parents linked the phone to the house, Dad had it at his business premises early in 1950. It was an ingenious method of keeping in touch with your neighbours in the district. Ultimately, it extended across Australia, giving birth to the PMG-PostMaster General's Department, which later became known as Telstra as it is today. A telephone book with a person's name, address, and phone number in every district and city around the country could be purchased to make contact with the service provided by the PMG.

The telephone created many new jobs that were nonexistent in previous decades. Telephone technicians installed and repaired the cables, engineers ensured the jobs were completed to specification, and linesmen installed the wires in the street and on overhead lines that had been installed when electricity was first connected.

Mobile phones were not invented then, but we children had our means of telecommunication and radio links. We used to punch a hole in the middle of one end of an opened used fruit or jam tin and thread a fishing line to another tin, similarly, at a fair distance apart. A match stick held the fishing line in the tin so it did not break through the hole. There, it was possible, and still is, to talk into one tin and hear the voice at the other end of the tin. Try it!

The other miracle was the magic of a crystal set. We could create the simplest radio receivers made with a few inexpensive parts, such as a wire for an antenna, a coil of wire, a capacitor that stored electric energy in a circuit, a crystal detector, and an earphone. We would listen to local radio stations when not allowed on the home radio. When I went to boarding school, listening to the radio was even more limited, mainly after we were sent to bed in our dormitory and the radio was switched off early. So it was not long before we boys constructed crystal sets to listen to our favourite music and radio plays when we were supposed to sleep. Grandad was a naughty boy back then.

Plenty of interesting things around the neighbourhood disappeared with the innovation and changes that occurred when I became a teenager. However, gramophones and radiograms were still in use in my early childhood. Our old neighbour Mrs McCudden had a gramophone, an old record player. These days, a gramophone is a genuine antique. A gramophone, like a cassette player, CD player, or MP3 player, is a device for playing music. A gramophone plays records: discs with grooves amplified by a needle. The sound is created solely by vibrations and requires no electrical setups. The gramophone would store sound in reverse by playing music with a horn-like device for listening, and the sounds would be consolidated in a diaphragm. You could see the needle making waves as it moved to create vibrations. It was the purest sound recording and had clarity ahead of its time. It was the era of sound waves, which operated like the waves of the ocean, whereas today, we have digital technology, which is more like the rhythms of the heart. An up-and-down sound motion, like peaks and troughs. If it seems confusing from Grandad's exclamation, then Google it!

Another fun thing we did as children was breed silkworms. They are not worms but moths. They produce the lava that forms silk. The famous "silk" that the insect produces is spun to make their cocoons. Each cocoon may contain a single strand of silk that is one and a half kilometres long! We would take from the cocoon the silk threads woven inside as silkworms. Using a cotton reel with five small hooks at the top, we used a technique like sewing with needle and thread to make things like silk cloth. We used to feed the silkworms mulberry leaves until they turned into butterfly moths and flew away. You can learn a lot more about this hobby on Google, too!

In early childhood, many things in the everyday household didn't exist as they do today, including refrigeration. Keeping food cool and fresh in a hot climate meant storing provisions in an ice chest. I mentioned this when I spoke of my Nana and Pop's meat safety in a previous chapter. It was like a small refrigerator that depended on a large block of ice to keep it cold. Once a week, the iceman arrived with a truck full of ice blocks. He used a claw-like metal holder to grip the ice block, which was about the size of twenty house bricks, and carried it to our ice chest. The ice blocks were placed in a large drawer or metal chest with a compartment at the top. Cold air fell and cooled the food below it. Ice boxes needed more ice every day or two, and the iceman would return for another block as regularly as clockwork. Later, Dad took an agency for what was known as a Defender refrigerator. It ran on an electric motor powered by kerosene and had radiator-like coils filled with gas at the back. The gas in the coils circulated like water does in a car radiator to keep it cool. The kerosene would burn, and a chimney at the rear collected the soot, which had to be cleaned out at least once a week. I was never happier than when the modern-day refrigerator replaced those kerosene-driven motors with electricity.

Another regular service was the 'Dunny man.' Growing up in a township before sewerage, one became accustomed to the delights of the outside toilet, commonly called the dunny. The name originated from an ancient word, dunnekin, meaning earth closet or cesspit. We also called it the long drop, the crapper, or the bog, but 'Dunny Can' became the most popular.

The dunny was a humble wooden box with a door that you closed by turning a wooden toggle, galvanised tin roofing, a wooden seat, a large tin can underneath, and a hinged door at the back. A nail to hang the dunny paper, made up of squares of torn newspaper, completed the setup. A good dunny usually offered something interesting to read. The Dunny Can Man came around about once a week to remove the entire can and leave us with a clean replacement, washed out with phenol. The piercing scent of phenol still evokes memories; it clung to your clothes, making anyone inside who had just used the can acutely aware of it! However, the most vivid memory is of preparing myself for the sprint back inside in the dark and the clever act I put on, pretending that no boogie man or slimy monster was chasing me as I fumbled with the house's back door.

The only home service that came to the door was the butcher. When Mum went to town to get fresh meat, it was always wrapped in white paper. Using white paper in the toilet was a pleasant change, as the ink from newspapers left stains on one finger and on the backside as well.

So we had regular visits from the baker with his horse-drawn wagon and supply of fresh bread. The fruit and vegetable man came from a nearby farm to supply us. The milkman arrived daily with fresh milk poured from a large jug to Mum's bottles in the refrigerator. I took an after-school job working for the apple man for extra money. We went from door to door selling apples by the bucket during the season. Likewise, I sometimes help the milkman deliver milk. Later, when it became pasteurised, it was sent to another town for processing. Then, I rode the milk wagons to collect large tins of milk from the dairy farmers and deliver it to the factory, where it was converted into bottled milk. Even then, a milk bottle had at least a cup full of cream floating on the top of the milk. The quality far surpassed the milk we buy from the supermarket today.

Dad was always away at work except at weekends. Dad's only domestic duties seem to be sharpening the axe, cutting wood for the fire from a pile stacked out back, knocking the head off a chock or two, plucking the feathers, and cleaning the bird for Sunday lunch. There was no plumbing or drainage in those days, and cooking was done with lard, of which the excess ended up down the drain, collecting in the grease trap under the house below the kitchen floor. This job was relegated to one of Dad's duties. Of course, being a mechanic, he was used to grease, so cleaning the trap was not an unpleasant chore for him.

My duties included collecting eggs from the chicken coop, but Mum always seemed there to do most of the chores. Getting water back then meant pumping it by hand from an overflow underground stream to the surface of an above-ground tank. Mum was undoubtedly relieved to see it rain as it saved her all that pumping and carrying water, and nature would then replenish the tank outside our backdoor and revive the vegetable patch. An old chip heater had to be filled with water at the head of the bathtub, and once fired up, the water would heat. A tap at its base could be turned on to add hot or cold water to a bath. It was standard practice to bathe in only a few centimetres of water as it was considered a precious commodity. The water was brought to a boil for cooking and washing our clothes by hand. The practice of boiling the old copper to wash, wringing the clothing by hand, and then pegging it all out to dry on a propped-up cloth line out in the backyard was the norm for my mother. As the song of the times went: "Monday is washing day… is everybody happy, you bet your life we are." Every day of the week, there were full-time chores to do, and we all took it in our stride, believing that it was how it was meant to be. It went with the territory, which I think was meant to be.

I feel sure my Dad spent so much time away from home building his empire and drinking with mates because, like me, he figured he didn't fit in at home. He considered himself having completed his duty as father, breadwinner, and provider, as far as he could take it.

It was also my duty to mow the lawns once a week with an old two-stroke motor. It meant ensuring the blades were sharp and the petrol and oil were mixed in the right volume. A spring-loaded reel held a cord, allowing it to be pulled out and retracted by a spring to start the mower. The spring tension effectively turned the "recoil" system, which was essential to pull the cord back in after each pull. It took some strength to pull the cord and start that damn thing. The mowing was the easy part.

It was also my duty to wash the family car before I could do what I liked for the remainder of the weekend. Parents did not worry so much about our safety back then. We were told to be home by nightfall and never questioned about what we did with our day. My friends and I always headed for the bush to play, climb trees, collect birds' eggs for another hobby, or kill a lizard or two just for fun. Of course, I would never do that today, knowing what I do about saving our wildlife and environment. We also took time to swim at a nearby beach or go upriver to catch fish. There is so much more I could share with you about those times, but enough of the reality of my childhood. It's time now for some more make-believe.

So here is some more space for you to do more drawings.

CHAPTER 5.

FROG STORIES

During my youth, there was a folk singer named Pete Seeger. He wrote his songs and sang them in concert halls and to schoolchildren. His songs featured animals and bush scenes; some read like favourite books. Here is one of his stories about a bullfrog.

"Once upon a time, a farmer walked down the road, playing his guitar and whistling a tune. He scratches his head and wishes he had words to the song. Then, he comes to a brook and leans on the bridge's railing. He sees a green bullfrog hopping left to right, from one bank to the other. The bullfrog looks up, sees the farmer, splashes into the mud, and gets dirty. As the farmer thinks of words for the chords, he plays on his guitar. Twang! Twang! Twang! The farmer laughs and sings a short token song.

The farmer walks down the road again, feeling proud of himself for making the lyrics for the song, and goes to the corner store to buy groceries. Hearing the farmer sing, the shopkeeper asks if he could teach him the new music. At first, the farmer refuses, so the shopkeeper tells the farmer to go home, but the farmer decides otherwise and teaches the song. While the farmer sings the song about the foolish frog, the shopkeeper enjoys it and decides to give everyone a party, passing strawberry-flavoured bubbling mineral water and potato chips for free as they dance by stamping on the floor.

At home, the farmer's wife tells the children to go to the corner store because she thinks the farmer is wasting his time as usual. The children run to the Corner Store and sing the farmer's song as they dance, drink mineral water, and eat potato chips. Then, the mothers, who held a frying pan in their hands, intent on hitting some sense into their farmer husbands' heads, forgot about being angered, dropped the pan, walked into the corner store, sang the song, drank bubbling mineral water, ate the potato chips, and danced.

The cows in the barn wonder where everybody is and say they are supposed to be milked, but they get very uncomfortable without any people around them. Hence, the cows walk out of the barns into the store, mooing the farmer's foolish frog song, dancing, drinking mineral water and eating potato chips. The hungry chickens then wonder where everybody is since they are supposed to be fed. They walk into the store, back to the song, dance, drink the sparkling water, and eat potato chips.

The barns "feel so empty", so they "squeeze" into the Corner Store and "creak" the song. Then, the grass, feeling lonely without the cows, goes into the Corner Store and "swishes" the song. After this, the brook of water does not have anything to bubble between, so the brook of water goes into the corner store, bubbling the song up and down the stairs. Everyone throws a big party, dancing and singing the song of the bullfrog who fell in the mud, drinking the free strawberry bubbling mineral water, and eating the free potato chips..

The bullfrog is now mid-air; the only things left are the road and the corner store. The bullfrog hops down the road, sees the corner store, hears the song about him, and becomes so proud that he "puffs" himself up with pride until he explodes in "all directions. The explosion causes everything and everyone to be propelled into the air, floating back down to their usual places. The farmer, his wife, and their children sit down to eat supper, feeling foolish about themselves.

The following day, the farmer, his wife, and their children set out to find the bullfrog. They searched high and low but found only empty bottles and potato chip packets in every direction—yet they did not see the bullfrog. The farmer then sang the song again, asked everyone he met if they knew how to whistle, and whistled the music as the end credits rolled like a film on a movie screen.

Here is another story about a hip frog, and we'll pick up on it now. A frog is on the way out to do some dancing and swinging. You'll be able to tell that he's a big mover, so you can start singing along.

"Frog went a-courtin', and he did go, uh-huh
Frog went a-courtin', and he did go, uh-huh
Frog went a-courtin', and he did go
To the Coconut Grove for the midnight show
Uh-huh, uh-huh, uh-huh,

Mollie Mouse was the hat-check girl, woo-woo
(He knew it all the time)
Mollie Mouse was the hat-check girl, woo-woo
Mollie Mouse was the hat-check girl
He thought he'd give this chick a whirl
Woo-woo, woo-woo, woo-woo

He sauntered up to Mollie Mouse's side, uh-huh
(The direct approach)
He sauntered up to Mollie Mouse's side, uh-huh
When he got up to Mollie Mouse's side
He whispered, "Mollie, will you be my bride?"
Uh-huh, uh-huh, uh-huh

Not without my Uncle Rat's consent, uh-uh
(Her uncle wrestles on TV)
Not without my Uncle Rat's consent, uh-uh
Not without my Uncle Rat's consent
I wouldn't marry the President
Uh-uh, uh-uh, uh-uh

Well, she said, "That's it, Clyde, better hit the road, farewell
That's it, Clyde, better hit the road, goodbye
That's it, Clyde, better hit the road
You ain't no frog. You're a horny toad
Farewell, goodbye, adios."

"Farewell, goodbye, adio.,
Farewell, goodbye, adios."

And here is another story that Grandad made up :

Now, here is a tale of two little toads,
 hopping along a dusty road,
as fate would have it on that day,
they drank too much booze,
fell in a hole.

The hole was deep, and it was dark,
they screamed and shouted,
 their throats were parched,
and they began to lose heart.

Their attitudes were turning blue,
 jumping and shouting,
scratched their heads, too,
they didn't know what to do!

Then, suddenly, without warning,
a group of frogs
came to their calling.
(Frogs are like that.)

The toads kept jumping,
and scrambling, too,
trying to
get out of the hole.

The frogs had no one
to pull them out,
so they just cried,
"Give up your shouting."

"Holy smokes!
nothing we can do,
give up the ghost,
You will die soon."

These frogs
they didn't understand
with a positive view
Toads can do anything!

Now, one of the toads,
took it all in,
stopped trying to jump,
and just croaked,
there and then.

The other toad,
despite frogs' negative shout,
would not give in, He wanted out.

So, despite the call,
to pack it in,
 The toad found strength,
from well within.

And so this toad,
despite frogs' hostile shouts,
climbed and climbed,
until he was out.

The crowd of frogs,
just gathered around,
they just could not
Understand.

They ask the toad,
why he did not give in,
despite their calls,
to pack it in.

The toad said quietly,
"I am deaf, you see,
I thought you were,
just cheering me on."

Then he said:

"So I just found,
some extra strength,
because I thought,
you supported me."

The moral to this little tale,
make sure you listen,
 to your Higher self,
not the rabble frogs.

The rabble frogs may
think you will fail,
but you can make it,
if you inhale.

The proof is here,
it's plain to see,
Cane toads,
multiply continuously.

It's built into their DNA,
an old bullfrog
 in a guru way,
told this Cain toad,
the state of play.

So listen to your Guru,
(that is your Higher self within)
with the steps you'll see,
he'll teach you to listen,
, you will see.

When you drink half a glass of water,
 just check it out before you swallow
and remember, you can either look at life like a glass half empty
Or take the positive approach of a glass half full

(That's your Grandad's philosophy.)

Finish this chapter by drawing a picture of a Cane toad here!

CHAPTER 6.

ANOTHER GRANDAD STORY

The main characters of this story had to learn some hard lessons because they did some naughty things that would have affected their physical and mental health if they had not listened to sound advice.

So the story starts with a small lizard walking along a bush track whistling a happy tune. Her name is Lizzy, and she is rocking from side to side as she moves her legs forward slowly. She is in no hurry to get where she is going. Besides, it's a hot day, and the sun is beating down with burning energy. Lizzy has no plans except to enjoy a pleasant walk, so she stops in the shade of a eucalyptus tree to rest. Looking up at the tree, Lizzy sees an old friend nestled in the fork of a branch. It's Krazy Koala who is always up to some mischief at a time when koalas are usually resting.

Lizzie smells smoke, looks up, and sees that it's coming from where Krazy Koala rests at the tree's fork. " What are you up to, Koala?" says Lizzie. In a half-dazed state, Krazy replies: " I'm smoking some grass." Lizzie responds: " I thought you Koalas only eat eucalyptus leaves." Koala, now in an unreal state of mind, hears sounds that don't exist and is not thinking straight. " Well, it's different, " says Koala:
"Why don't you come up and join me?" Lizzie, in her unthinking way, is unaware of the dangers of smoking grass and joins Koala to try this weed. After some time passes, Lizzie realises she is getting very thirsty due to one

of the side effects of smoking Koala's silly weed. She notices that Krazy Koala hears noises that aren't real and starts saying ridiculous things like, "I can hear music, and did you hear that bear growl?" Since Lizzie hadn't smoked much of the grass, she knew what Krazy said was nonsense. So, she makes her way down to the river to get a drink. Lizzie leans over the riverbank and splashes. She falls headfirst and nearly drowns.

As luck would have it, Snappy crocodile is nearby and lifts Lizzy onto the river bank. " What happened to you?" says the crocodile. "Well, I was smoking grass with Krazy Koala and got thirsty, so I came here for a drink. How was I to know that wacky weed would make me dizzy, too? " Snappy crocodile becomes angry. " Where is that Krazy Koala now? " He says. Lizzy points the way, so Snappy heads up the track to where Krazy talks to non-existent voices. " Hey, Koala!" yells Snappy to Koala, who looks down and gets a big fright, for he thinks in his unreal state that Snappy is Lizzy. " Struth!" He exclaims: " How much water did you drink?"

Snappy crocodile is in no mood for Krazy Koala's foolish behaviour and orders him to come down from the tree. By this time, Lizzy arrived on the scene. Snappy begins to lecture Krazy Koala and Lizzie Lizard on the dangers of smoking grass. " This stuff is for dopes; it is why it is sometimes called that…dope."
" Now I know why you are called Krazy. This stuff will cause you forever to lose your mind, think you hear voices and sounds that are not real and cause irreversible damage to your health. " So Snappy got Krazy Koala to promise he

would not go near that wacky weed again. And Krazy crossed his heart and promised he never would again. And so did 'Dizzy Miss Lizzy.

So Snappy Crocodile reminded Krazy Koala that whilst eucalyptus leaves would continue to make him sleep a lot, he would not lose touch with reality like smoking that wacky weed did to him.

From that day forward, Krazy Koala called himself 'wise ' and taught other koalas that eating eucalyptus leaves makes them sleep a lot but doesn't make them "high and stupid".

He went to great lengths to explain how leaves are low in nutrients and high in fibre, which takes a lot of energy to digest. He assured them they didn't need to drink water as the leaves had plenty of moisture, so they could rest easy and relax more often in a fork of a eucalyptus tree, which also made all the koalas happy. As for Lizzy, she was no longer dizzy and never fell into the river again because she had more sense now and knew not to follow anyone else's lead unless it was in her best interest to do so.

The following rhyme comes from a distant past, but you will likely enjoy it.

The sun comes up, and the sun goes down.
The hands on the clock keep going around.
I get up, and it's time to lie down.
Life gets tough, doesn't it?

My shoe's untied, but I don't care.
I ain't-figurin' on goin' nowhere.
I'd have to wash and comb my hair.
That's just a wasted effort.

Water in the well is getting lower and lower.
Can't take a bath for six months or more
But I've heard it said, and it's true, I'm sure,
That too much bathing weakens you.

I open the door, and the flies swarm in.
I shut the door, and I was sweating again.
I move too fast, and I crack my shin.
Just one darn thing after t'other.

My old brown mule must be sick.
I jabbed him in the rump with a pin on a stick.
He humped his back, but he wouldn't kick.
There's somethin' cockeyed somewhere.

There's a mouse a-chain on the pantry door.
He's been at it for at least a month or more.
When he gets through, he'll surely be sore.
Cause There ain't a darn thing in there.

Hound dog howls; he's so forlorn.
The laziest dog that ever was born.
He's howlin' 'cause he's a-sittin' on a thorn —
just too tired to move off it.

The Tin roof leaks, and the chimney leans.
There's a hole in the seat of my old blue jeans.
And I've eaten the last of them, pork and beans.
I just can't depend on nothing.

Cow's gone dry, and the hens won't lay.
Fish quit biting last Saturday.
Troubles pile up, day by day —
Now I'm getting dandruff.

Grief and misery, pains and woes,
debts and taxes, and so on.
And I think I'm getting a cold in the nose …
A-choo! Ah, life gets tasteless, don't it?

Can you picture the old hut with the tin roof?

How about drawing a picture of the hut, dog, mouse, older man, or all of the characters in the story.

CHAPTER 7.

THE WAYS OF OLD

There is much to be said about the old way of life before communities were formed and people lived the bush way of life. The air was clean and fresh before motor vehicles carried people and transported food to supermarkets. People made clothing from animal skins and coats from sheep wool before clothing shops were ever thought of to purchase the fashions we liked. It was a time before we had houses and schools to learn the golden rules. When people got together, they had great conversations, sang, and danced before returning to isolation. Would you return to that way of life now? Let's take a little peek at the story of an old mentor who lived that way before that lifestyle ran out.

Pete Seeger, a folk singer, political activist, humanitarian, environmentalist, and patriarch, came from a pioneering family. His parents, Charles Seeger and Constance de Clyver Edson, advanced research in American folk music during the 1930s and greatly influenced his son's interests. Thus, it was natural for Pete to pursue his dreams in adulthood.

Now Pete, so he wouldn't get lonely, married a girl named Toshi Ohata. Her father was a Japanese exile from Shikoku, and her mother was a native American from Washington, D.C. They were a perfect match, and pretty soon, Pete built a rustic cabin on a wooden hilltop near Beacon, New York State. He built it in 1950 from logs he cut on the property where he and his wife, Toshi, lived and raised their family. The only other living things around were bears, squirrels, wombats, and wriggly things like snakes and lizards, as well as wild animals, birds like eagles that nested in the trees. So, from some trees he had grown, he collected fruit to eat, like apples, oranges, peaches, and pears. He and his wife learnt to grow vegetables near their cabin from seeds Pete gathered in the wild. In a nearby river were fish of all shapes and sizes, oysters, mussels, and fish he caught now and then and cooked them on an open fire. They did not need a tap for water to drink or to wash after a hard day hunting for food, for all the freshwater required was from the river. As for firewood, Pete cut branches from trees into logs for his open fireplace in the winter.

Now conscious of the environment, Pete caught only one of everything they needed to eat, not to upset the natural balance. This method of hunting was acceptable for decades when only a few whites, like Pete and his family, moved to the area. They followed the traditional ways of the native population and mixed well with their Indian brothers, often swapping food and supplies in exchange for what they needed. However, in the long run, that didn't work.

Imagine a time when you could sit on a log and be in tune with nature, birds, animals, and all living things. That was fine until more people came to live in the area. Some of these wanted to sit on the log, too. So more and more came to sit on that log until the one there first finally got pushed off the log and had nowhere else to go. So, the Indian natives headed for new horizons, moving to other mountains, and the same process happened again.

So let us go back to the people who lived in the Beacon's hills and valleys when the paleface (white man) first came to our land of the Indian peoples. Let us hear their story: "They arrived with pieces of paper that said they were entitled to take our land and that we could live in the mountains whilst they lived on the flat country. We did move to the mountains for many years, but in time, more and more white men came until they had taken over all the valley, and those that sold them the land were dead, and their sons had taken over, and when there was no land left they began to sell the land on the mountains. We tried to take them to court. We had white lawyers who pleaded our case, but there was no chance. We were just Indians. That's what they called us. Where would we go? There were Indians out west, but we did not know them, and in the north and the east, there were white people there too, so where would we go?

And so we went to the black people in the land they called Green Haven. We went to the black people and asked if we could live there, too. We will learn to be farmers because we didn't want to live with the white people as they did not understand us, but the black people did; the white people did not always treat us right, but the black people did. So that is why many people are Indian and part black man in GreenHaven.

So because many more people arrived, the hunting and trapping of animals and fish, or fruit from the trees soon ran out and like many others, Pete and his family were forced to go to the city and towns to buy supplies from the local tradespeople who transported supplies from far and wide and expected money instead of furs from animals or wild meat to pay for the supplies. Then more and more people arrived, supermarkets and big stores overran the tradespeople, and more and more children learned how to survive in a new world. That was fine when everybody was considered equal, but in time, that changed, and some people took control of others, and nobody was happy.

So the white men devised a plan to teach children how to live by their ' golden' rules, and they set up schools and universities to educate everyone; it was soon forgotten that we humans have individual personalities, and we each have a dream in our hearts to bring to life from our heartbeat, for our spirit and the benefit of others. Meanwhile, men unthinkingly encouraged farmers to grow mass crops, using processed seeds that had been genetically modified to produce more. The nutrition was inferior, so they added artificial fertilisers to boost crops that lacked nourishment. In addition, they bred many cows, sheep, and goats and encouraged chickens to lay too many eggs to feed many people who were still not happy. And that was not all; they dirtied the rivers and streams, caused the air to be filled with smog and used gas to run cars for people, to get to and from wherever they think they should be going. Trucks would run up and down the highways and byways, delivering unhealthy food, clothing, and other things to pollute the air further. So the rivers became even more polluted, the water became undrinkable, and the food eaten caused sickness. The sky grew dark with smog, and nobody could breathe fresh air anymore. Something had to be done, so people like Pete Seeger began to sing songs to encourage people to think and change things. He wanted to point out that we are conditioned not to think but to go along. In his mind, we were being put into little boxes and brainwashed to believe the same. Here are the words of his song, and if you can read behind the scenes, you will understand why they are essential.

Little boxes on the hillside
Little boxes made of ticky-tacky
Little boxes
Little boxes
Little boxes all the same

There's a green one and a pink one.
And a blue one and a yellow one
And they're all made out of ticky-tacky.
And they all look just the same.

And the people in the houses all go to the university.
And they all get put in boxes, little boxes all the same
And there are doctors, and there are lawyers.
And business executives are all made out of ticky-tacky, and they all look the same.

And they all play on the golf course and drink their martini dry. And they all have pretty children, and the children go to school. The children go to summer camp and then to university. They all get put in boxes and come out the same.

The boys go into business, marry, and raise a family. They are all put in boxes, little boxes, and are all the same.

There's a green one, and a pink one.
And a blue one and a yellow one
And they're all made out of ticky-tacky.
And they all look just the same.

We know children are more intelligent than adults, and you can see the mess adults have made. Well, not all parents are dummies; some are smarter than others. Holding on to the dreams within your heart and acting upon them is essential. You can follow your dream even though you may feel you don't belong in a little box like others have accepted. Grandad should qualify this by stating that we all have to live in the world as it now stands, including the education system, but we can still follow the beat of our hearts, the drummer you hear. A wise man once told me: "Everyone's heart beats to the tune of a different drummer. Let them follow the drummer that they hear." And on another occasion, he said: "The masses of men lead lives of quiet desperation." Both these statements your Granddad states here are the truth.

Well, back to Pete Seeger to see how one man fought to clean up the rivers, marched against wars for peace, and taught children how to sing again, think, and act in the best interest of each other and others.

When war broke out in the second decade of the twentieth century, Pete Seeger was scaled down in the army to be an engineer, but soon, he was singing songs to bolster the spirits of the troops. Once home again, he marched for peace and the people's Civic rights. Before too long, another war broke out, and Pete was too old to go to fight, but instead, he sang more songs to encourage peace and the futility of war because too many people died as a result, which was a waste. Another song of his that you will see happen repeatedly, and we don't get the message, do we?

Where have all the flowers gone?
Long time passing
Where have all the flowers gone?
Long time ago

Where have all the flowers gone?
Young girls have chosen men.
When will they ever learn?
When will they ever learn?

Where have all the young girls gone?
Long time passing
Where have all the young girls gone?
Long time ago

Where have all the young girls gone?
Gone to young men, everyone
When will they ever learn?
When will they ever learn?

Where have all the young men gone?
Long time passing
Where have all the young men gone?
Long time ago

Where have all the young men gone?
Gone to the soldiers every one,
When will they ever learn?
When will they ever learn?

Where have all the soldiers gone?
Long, long time passing
Where have all the soldiers gone?
Long time ago
Where have all the soldiers gone?
Gone to the graveyards every one,
When will they ever learn?
When will they ever learn?

Where have all the graveyards gone?
Long time passing
Where have all the graveyards gone?
Long time ago

Where have all the graveyards gone?
Gone to flowers everyone
When will they ever learn?
When will they ever learn?

Where have all the flowers gone? The young girls have picked everyone. When will they ever learn?

Pete continued to write songs and do work to help others. Sometimes, things worked out fine, like cleaning up the water on the Hudson River or marching for people's civil rights. Now and again, he would come up with a gem of a song like this one.

When we look and see
Things are not what they should be
God's counting on me
God's counting on you

When we look and see
Things are not what they should be
God's counting on me
God's counting on you

Hoping we'll all pull through
Hoping we'll all pull through
Hoping we'll all pull through
Me and you

It's time to turn things around.
Trickle up, not trickle down.
God's counting on me
God's counting on you

It's time to turn things around.
Trickle up, not trickle down.
God's counting on me
God's counting on you.

Hoping we'll all pull through
Hoping we'll all pull through
Hoping we'll all pull through

And when the oil men keep on drilling
And when they drill, baby, drill
Leads to another spill, baby, spill

God's counting on me; God's counting on you.

Grandad's writings may not be relevant now for you as they are for me in this old world, but one day, you may reread these words, and in your own time of wisdom and old age, you will see that the cycle of life continues until we learn the lesson for the mutual benefit of all.

So perhaps we should finish this chapter with a song called ' The River that flows both ways.'

Once, the Sachems told a story of a land where great spirits were blessed. The people followed the legend of the great waters in the West. They stopped where they found that the fishing was good.

Earth was fertile, and the rivers ran in the woods.

And now, I could be happy spending my days on the river that flows both ways.

I could be happy spending my days on the river that flows both ways.

So here is some history of how the cycle of life evolved.

" First came the trappers catching their fill; it went to the traders. Good fortune they found, and the people and the valleys were kind.

So the farmers soon followed closely behind, with shops laden with flowers from Yonkers, seed for the pastures, and corn.

Then came the writers and painters, who wrote of beauty, whilst the painters did paint, and singers sang songs of the river and stories, kept alive the old river's lore

The sun is setting golden over the Palisades ,
the afternoon ends, and daylight fades.

And it could be the starlight, the moon reflecting in Haverstraw Bay, or the fog rolling down from the highlands at the break of a brand-new day.

But apple cider, pumpkins, Strawberries, and other fruits make the people of the river glad they were born.

Oh! I could be happy just spending my days on the river that flows both ways. Oh! I could be satisfied spending my days on the river that flows both ways. "

Rick Nether sang this song with school kids on the Tomorrow Children album, credited to Pete Seeger with the Rivertown Kids and Friends. A group of friends, Captain Dick Marley, Rick Nether, Leonard Lipton and Donna Nestler, formed a Ferry Sloop incorporation and sailed the Sloop Sojourner Truth' from Hastings, New York, and the boat met its demise on the rocks in a storm in 2002. The Ferry Sloop organisation is still active, and a white fibreglass boat was sailed mid-These days.

Since Pete Seeger dedicated the piece, the farmers market outgrew the Beacon Sloop Club and moved to Main Street, and the 'Something to Say Cafe' ended when kids who ran it got older and went off to college or took jobs. But the Beacon Sloop Club remains vibrant with monthly events, music jams and festivals. In 2014, the park north of the club was officially named the Pete and Josh Seeger Riverfront Park. In Cleaning up the Hudson River, a few decades or so before this, the sloop 'Clearwater' with Pete D. Rick Nestler and David Bertz built it on the back of the demise of the sloop 'So Journey Truth' disaster.

They sailed the Clearwater Sloop, mainly due to environmental issues, to clean up the Hudson River. The Hudson River Clearwater has always been a singing boat, and Pete was well known for concerts and festivals up and down the river. Many singing groups were filmed. As a result, the most notable among these was the absinthe Hudson River Sloop Singers. The group disbanded in the 1990s but got together for the Clearwater annual fundraising gathering of the larger Clearwater community. There was also the Walkout Chorus, which was just as popular.

The Sloop Singers and the Walkabout Chorus are just two support organisations formed around Clearwater over the years. Others include the Riverlovers in the Croton-Cissing area, fiery Sloops in southern Westchester, New York City Friends of Clearwater, New Jersey Friends of Clearwater, and up near

Albany, the North River Friends of Clearwater. Many of these groups have followed the Beacon Sloop Club model of having monthly meetings with a potluck supper following singing.

The song The River That Flows Both Ways has been sung up and down the Hudson for the past four decades since 1980, and Pete Seeger's version has always been the most popular.

Here is another one from Pete, which I am sure you will like:

This little light of mine, I'm gonna let it shine.
This little light of mine, I'm gonna let it shine.
This little light of mine, I'm gonna let it shine.
Let it shine, let it shine, let it shine.

Everywhere I go, I'm gonna let it shine.
Everywhere I go, I'm gonna let it shine.
Everywhere I go, I'm gonna let it shine
. Let it shine, let it shine, let it shine.

This little light of mine, I'm gonna let it shine.
This little light of mine, I'm gonna let it shine.
This little light of mine, I'm gonna let it shine.
Let it shine, let it shine, let it shine.

We will sing in peace; we will sing in harmony.
We will sing in peace; we will sing in harmony.
We will sing in peace; we will sing in harmony.
We will sing in peace; we will sing in harmony.

This little light of mine, I'm gonna let it shine.
Let it shine, let it shine, let it shine.

Let it shine around the world;

We're gonna let it shine. Let it shine, let it shine!

Draw a picture of this little light of mine here as it relates to your little light..

CHAPTER 8.

A LITTLE MORE ON GRANDAD

In contemplating the life of my Granddad and my Father, I have drawn some interesting conclusions about my life and times of childhood. Equally, the influences of my Irish forebears, folk singers like Peter Seeger, my attitude to life in my younger years and how I once lived still resonates with me today. It is not difficult to draw on some comparisons of my own and draw a template of my youth to my now old age. I trust you will bear with the telling here, for it is for your ears that I might say that I have gained some wisdom in my life; when it is set and done, I know little, but it has been a good life upon reflection.

I grew up on the Nambucca River and witnessed many changes in the natural environment and economically in the years before I reached my teens. I witnessed bushfires, cyclones, river floods, famine and sometimes unbearable suffering, which, when I look back on it, all made me more resilient to acceptance of life on life's terms. In my preschool years, most local transports were by horse and cart. All the roads were dirt tracks, including the main Pacific Highway, which wound along the coast from Sydney to Brisbane before the government of the day in 1950 began to widen the lanes to more than one each way. Interestingly, it took my entire lifetime before it was finished to four lanes and bypassed most towns along the routes North and South.

Entertainment in my pre-boarding school days comprised the annual agricultural show, Ashton's Circus, which arrived by train before the Big Top tent was erected on the local sports ground. A parade of elephants, followed by caged lions, tigers, hyenas, and trapeze artists on swings, clowns juggling balls, and a band of marching girls with painted faces and masks dressed in pretty skirts and displaying long legs ventured through the main street of the town on the way to the park to erect the massive tent for an overnight circus before packing up the next day and moving on to the next town. The local School of Arts often held a continual flow of singers and plays. Watching movies was a Saturday afternoon of imaginative joy as two feature films were shown, a couple of cartoons, and a series of shorts, and our main outlet for this was two decades before TV came to Australia. Our other outlets attended local sports events or participated in tennis, squash, and rugby league. Apart from collecting bird eggs or silkworms, which I've previously mentioned, the nearby beaches were always at our beck and call.

Your Granddad was sometimes a naughty boy, too. For example, when I took an apple from a neighbour's tree that overhung our side of the fence, my mother caught me eating it and chastised me for stealing what was not mine. She marched me off to the neighbour's front door and knocked. Old Mister Casey listened as I justified my reasons for eating one of his apples. He listened attentively whilst, under penalty of punishment from my mother, announced my apology. The old gentleman congratulated me for telling the truth and announced that whenever I wanted an apple, strawberry or melon from his garden, I only needed to ask, and I could eat my fill. I left that day with two lessons; " ask and you shall receive" and "Honesty is the best policy."

Of course, that was not my only wayward act. My good friend Des and I, apart from doing our bush tracking and learning bush ways from the local Aboriginals, had another favourite game. We sometimes amused ourselves by leaving a two-pound note, equivalent to around five dollars in today's money, on the main highway tied to a long fishing line. Once the line was rolled out of the road, we hid on the edge of the bush, holding the other end and waited for a passing car to spot the money on the road. As soon as the driver got out of the car to pick up the money, we quickly pulled in the fishing line, and the driver usually stood in the middle of the road scratching his head, wondering how on earth the money vanished, then the driver disappeared too. That all worked fine until a smatter driver ran faster than we could wind in the fishing line. He picked up the money, disconnected the fishing line, and walked off, calling " Thank You." So our game was up, so to speak, and it meant we had to find another game of chance. It wasn't long before we raced each other in billy carts we made from old wooden crates. We added wheels to the back, tied a rope to a cross and two front wheels for steering. In the old days, carts like these were a necessary accompaniment to a boy's life. Descendants of goat carts (hence the name 'billy' cart), these long-handled boxes on wheels were used for family errands, newspaper runs, and hauling whatever boys liked to haul around. The best fun was racing down hills in these out-of-control carts. Many a skinned knee and gravel rash on our hands resulted from riding those carts. As the saying goes, 'Boys will be boys!"

In those first twelve years of my life, I witnessed the vast business change in the district, with sawmills being erected for the ever-growing need for housing as immigrants began to pour into our once quiet little sleepy hollow. The following changes include mechanisation, and people like my father capitalise on selling and servicing motor vehicles and machinery. Soon, the old businesses were overtaken by modern shops, and not so long after, supermarkets replaced the cooperative and general stores. When I headed to boarding school, the township had a small factory, meatworks and a network of milk supply trucks delivering milk from cans to bottles. Suppliers no longer came to our home's door with food or medicinal supplies. No longer did the dunny man come to change the can, did Dad need to clean out the grease trap or chop wood for the fire, did Mum have to pump water to the tank outside the door to draw water, boil the copper to wash clothing and hang it all out to dry on the line out back. We had a washing machine and hot and cold running water and a clothes dryer. Not just a bathtub but a shower and a press-button toilet! Meals were not dependent on lighting the wood smoking fuel stove either, for we had an electric oven and refrigeration to keep food cool. And to my joy, we, at long last, had a TV set.

It took until the early 1960s for this to all transpire, but the changes for a young man hardly through his teens, after five years away at boarding school, came with lightning speed and the light of the changes to my delight. It was the time of rock n'roll, Elvis Presley, Chuck Berry, Bill Haley and the Comets, and country and western music, which still resisted change until the explosion of Beatlemania! Beatlemania was the fanaticism surrounding the English rock band The Beatles from 1963 to 1966. The group's popularity grew in the United Kingdom in late 1963 and worldwide, propelled by the singles "Please Please Me", "From Me to You" and "She Loves You". You can check them out on Google if you will.

My reconnection with folk music started when Pete Seeger sang in concert at the Sydney Town Hall in 1964. It inspired me to go on stage with another singer as a duet, singing the Everly Brothers' songs, the best of Pete Seeger's, and other folk singers' songs. We won a Millers Pub competition for our singing act, which entertained us in concert halls. Of course, this was a long time ago, and Grandad is probably too old to go back and try all that again, but let me tell you a secret... I would like to!

Some young men go mad in their single days, and need the influence of a woman to settle them down. It took a while before your Granddad came to his senses. I tried everything from flying upside down in a small aeroplane to riding high up on the mast of a Russian ship in a cyclone. I also attempted to enter the boxing ring against a well-known English boxer in the best of a three-round bout. He had never lost a fight, and Grandad got a draw in this match. However, he did not have a mark on him, and silly old me had a split lip, a black eye and a headache. Lesson learnt after the event.

In my primary school years, I captained our school's North Coast Rugby League football team, and we won the competition against all towns as far south as Wingham and north of Coffs Harbour. By the time I got to boarding school I was no longer the top football player. Grandad didn't grow to be tall and was no longer fast on his feet, whereas the rest of my team outgrew me. I persisted in continuing to play right up until two years after I left school. I loved team sports, but I suffered because of my efforts. Head injuries resulted in repeated concussions and torn shoulder ligaments that took ages to fix. Another lesson learnt after the event. In hindsight, I should have been a ball boy or a referee! [Both your Dad and Uncle Sam were exceptionally talented Rugby Union football players in their school years, but they had the sense not to continue to play as they got older.]

Like most people in life, your grandad had his ups and downs. We sometimes forget that we have lived most of our lives with our ladder against the wrong wall. In such situations, our hearts rule our heads in the long run, and we become right to our true purpose in life. Grandad ran hard for many years for a family fortune in the business world. I was like Pete Seeger sang about in the Little Boxes song I mentioned earlier. I had sold my soul to the work-a-day world for what I believed was right for me at the time, but it never was.

When my life went pear-shaped, I lost everything: marriage, family, business and many fair-weather friends. One soon realises that half the world doesn't love you but the other half does, and it doesn't matter anyway. No longer having family commitments or a company and home to maintain, I set out with a knapsack on my back and a sleeping bag, and I lived a free life after that. While on one of my many adventures, I discovered I could write books and songs. It was the destiny of my heart that I had long before lost touch with; now, after having written over twenty-three books and three albums of songs, I am doing as nature and the universe intend me to do. So remember to follow your dreams and the feelings within your heart and not what others may think you should do. It all works out in the end, and if it's not working out as you may expect right now, then it's not the end. Check out Grandad's Sons on YouTube's Top Songs Doug McPhillips, and you may get a glimpse into your old granddad's head. Also, go to caminoway.com.au/books to view my stories.

One of Grandad's lyrical songs offers a glimpse into where he once was and where he now exists.

O'Gormans' by the fire.

When the sun shines on the mountain,
You can see a little town,
were the children playing in the dream time,
where happiness was born.

Scattered memories in the dreaming,
visions of some distant scene,
Come to me now in the midnight hour,
shades of smoke in this misty dream.

Loving memories of fun and laughter,
flash across the flaming night,
forging family lifetime memories,
whilst the children sing their tunes.

Run inside,
sit with your dreams by the fireside,
run inside,
new dreams can still be born.

In those days of wine and roses
were friendships once bound,
scattered memories fill the mind now,
by the hearth and flaming fire!

Oh! the night was turning black,
as the flames grew higher and higher,
and the embers turn to golden stars,
at O'Gormans by the fire!
Yeah, we had so many good times,
great friendships way back when,
singing children and stories telling,
at O'Gormans by the fire.!

Run inside,
sit with your dreams by the fireside,
run inside,
new dreams can still be born.

Oh! The flames were rising higher,
when the night was closing in,
we drank wine with whisky chasers,
and we stayed warm by the fire.

When the sun shines on the mountain,
You can see a little town,
smoke rising from the chimneys,
where the fireside hearth dies down.

People out there in the village morn,
on their way to daily chores,
facing bitter cold and sleet now,
dressed up to keep them warm.

Run inside,
sit with your dreams by the fireside,
run inside,
new dreams can still be born.

Mist is rising from a night,
all is quiet, and the air is clean,
in the little village hamlet,
where once I lived out my dreams.

Oh! I awake now, stretching and yawning,
from the wonder of my dream,
shattered memories and desolation,
of a life that's forever gone.

Run inside,
sit with your dreams by the fireside,
new dreams can still be born.

Oh! The days of wine and roses,
and our life in fields of dreams,
distant recall of golden friendships,
fading memories of fireside scenes.

Run inside,
sit with your dreams by the fireside,
Run inside,
New dreams can still be born.

We had so many good times,
questioning life and what it means,
times of rounding, roping and riding,
in our worn-out boots and jeans.

Oh! I take to the road singing,
plucking on my old banjo,
singing this song of distant memories,
of loves now lost in dreams.

Run inside,
sit with your dreams by the fireside,
run inside,
new dreams can still be born.

Run inside,
sit with your dreams by the fireside,
run inside,
new dreams can still be born.

CHAPTER 8.

THE FINALE

When the mother Eagle hatches her eggs in the nest, she nurtures the little ones until they are old enough to leave. Then she picks them up one at a time, flies high up into the sky, and drops the young one in the hope that it takes flight and thus begins its life on its journey. If the chick does not fly, the mother Eagle swoops down, regathers the chick, and flies high again and again until the chick finally takes flight. You may note that Mother Eagle, not Father Eagle, attends this task. Father eagles usually go out hunting for food to feed their mother and themselves before breeding a new batch of eagle eggs for hatching. He may also be the guard to protect the nest against other eagles attacking. Sometimes, the father eagle will gather straw and build another nest in a new location. To do so is if there is a danger of another predator or competing eagle seeking the former nesting spot. And the process of breeding, hatching, and sending the little ones on their way starts all over again.

Interestingly, humans don't naturally follow eagles' path in teaching their young to fly and sending them out to make their way in the world. We are much slower in learning to teach our children the ways of nature.

In time, we all have to face the inevitable fact that we have to face the slings and arrows of outrageous fortune and what life offers us. Any mother knows that the price of self-sacrifices is punctuated by a rude awakening at some point in time. It is the cycle of life that we have to grow into or deteriorate. We must change; we can't stand still. So begin now to enjoy every moment of your childhood, and know your mother or father's sacrifices for you so that you may grow. And always follow your heart's desire when it comes to using your talents for the greater good of all concerned. It is paramount to your growth that you create what you will for your pathway in life. It doesn't matter how it looks to somebody else. It only matters how it looks to you.

Within us is a higher self, a pure spirit of consciousness that instils us with knowledge and a divine light of undertaking to guide us through the darkness to a more excellent light. Therein lies the happiness that we come to believe in, act upon and live by. So you can be as happy as you decide to be. Achieve your aims and aspirations in the long run to the best of your abilities. So be brave, and do not be afraid to step out into the world and learn with the best you can offer. You may make mistakes, but they don't matter if you continue trying. You will find your footing in the world in a good time. Be brave, be grateful for the good things in your life, and know that your old grandad is here for you whenever you need him.

Your old grandad had many scars on his body and just as many in his heart, but they have all served to make me who I am today. Sometimes, in my striving, I've landed in a pothole in the road. And sometimes, I hit that pothole again. Ultimately, I have learned to remember that there is a pothole in the road, and I must remember to go around it to progress on my happy road to destiny. You, too, will have your challenges, potholes and difficulties. You progress and reach the dreams you desire by pushing onward, despite any barrier. Remember, it is not so much getting what you want; striving along the way makes it all worthwhile.

When grandad was a boy, push bikes became the rage and we rode our bikes everywhere, often far out on bush tracks and away from the town. We had fun racing each other up and down hills and did dangerous things too, which I would not advise anyone to do, like riding without holding onto the handlebars and using the legs to control the balance of the bike, or trying to stand up on the seat and keep balance without falling off. It was good luck that no wild country boys got injured. We also had fun making a bow and arrows and using a string or fishing line to attach to the bow to fire the arrow, hoping to kill a bird or lizard with the sharpened sticks we made as arrows. It was not until our teens that common sense came into play and we gained the wisdom of protecting things of nature and ceased killing anything. Lille girls were never that way, which is why you girls have always been known to be smarter than boys, but don't tell anyone I told you this, particularly boys.

So let me now finish up this little book with some truths that your granddad has learnt which you may wish to know:

In my boyhood, there was a saying: " Some guys tear through life like a wizard. Folks point him out and say, 'He's a wizard.' Then he's dead at forty with a burnt-out gizzard. Life gets tedious, doesn't it?"

Eventually, I felt compelled to slow down, which has made all the difference. Here are some other things I've learnt that have made some difference, too. I slept better when I brought a feather bed. I love being alone, surrounded by silence, and listening to my inner self. I came to realise that I am not so special but unique. I came to know that I am worthy to know a God of my understanding directly, and I can talk to Him, and he listens to me. I began to see that I didn't need to chase after life, because life came to me. I experience what God wants me to learn if I am quiet and still. The part of me that I had long ignored, the orphan of my soul, quit seeking attention and peace came to me. I grew more patient and calm once I realised that the heart's desires did come. That is, except when I forget.

When I lay still and scan my body with my eyes closed, I start feeling all my feelings. When I do that, something amazing happens. You should try it. You will see what I mean. When I am relaxed and accept life on its terms, I can equally accept joy and sorrow. When I get into the habit of practising meditation every day, a profound act of self-love comes to me. Whenever I feel anxious, angry, restless or sad, I discover who needs my love if I listen patiently. I no longer need people or things to make me happy. I no longer need people or things to make me feel safe. It is then I began to feel a divine presence in me. So that my inner heart becomes content and I can smile and laugh as I please.

And here is the funny part: When I think about my old granddad or my mother or father just before I go to sleep, I feel their presence there, and I sleep like a newborn baby, knowing I am being cradled in their arms.

These days, too, I listen to the wisdom of my own heart, and God speaks to me there. It is my intention, and he sometimes gives me a poem, a song to sing, or, more often than not, a whole story to write a new book. How amazing is that!

I am coming to the end of this little book. I hope you find it as beneficial as I have in writing it. I am leaving a couple of pages for you to draw your thoughts, dreams, and visions for the future. So, occasionally, think of your old grandad in your drawings, dreams, or stories. Know that he will always inspire you in your dreams, and you will also be an inspiration in his.

Doug McPhillips, poet, singer, songwriter, and author, began his journey of discovery over a decade ago after having had life-changing experiences.

The many tracks he has traversed throughout the Northern Hemisphere and down under in New Zealand and Australia have resulted in the facts and fiction of this novel.

Doug has written twenty novels, two books of poems, a travel guide and three albums of his songs, all inspired by his adventures.

www.ingramcontent.com/pod-product-compliance
Lightning Source LLC
Chambersburg PA
CBHW061750070526
44585CB00025B/2853